THIS IS THE LIBERTINES QUIZBOOK

The Quizbook is intended to taleer of The Libertines (All information :tober 2024)

It starts from the early beginnin igh to the present day.

The book includes sections of multiple-choice questions. In between the multiple-choice questions there will be a lyrics quiz based on each of the band's albums

There will also be questions relating to recordings the band members made away from The Libertines

Each section can be cross referenced against the answers provided towards the end of the book.

Grab a drink, a pencil, put on some tunes and enjoy the quizbook – or take it to your friends and fill out together – quiz your best mate who claims to know everything about The Libertines and see how much they truly know.

Most of all – enjoy the journey of this band from small intimate gigs to headline tours.

B Demure

The Libertines Quizbook

Contents

THE LIBERTINES

Early Days

1. Peter and Carl initially started the band under what name?

    a) The Change ☐

    b) The Start ☐

    c) The Chart ☐

    d) The Strand ☐

2. Who was the original third member of this band?

    a) Pete Bedlow ☐

    b) Steve Short ☐

    c) Steve Bedlow ☐

    d) Pete Short ☐

3. The band changed their name to The Libertines - inspired by "Lusts of the Libertines" by which French writer?

    a) Marquis de Sade ☐

    b) Victor Hugo ☐

    c) Albert Camus ☐

    d) Honore de Balzac ☐

4. Which member of Razorlight played bass for The Libertines for a short period of time?

    a) Andy Burrows ☐

    b) Carl Dalemo ☐

    c) Shian Smith ☐

    d) Johnny Borrell ☐

5. Which bar in Islington did Doherty work as a barman? The band would also play numerous gigs here

    a) Filthy McNastys ☐

    b) The Lexington ☐

    c) The Grace ☐

    d) The Ladybird Bar ☐

6. Who was appointed as the first manager of the band? Although just for a six-month period

    a) Ian Morton ☐

    b) Roger Morton ☐

    c) Roger Peterson ☐

    d) Ian Peterson ☐

7. Gary joined the band on drums in 2000 - who did he replace due to being deemed "too old"?

    a) Craig Blanchett ☐

    b) Paul Blanchett ☐

    c) Craig Dufour ☐

    d) Paul Dufour ☐

8. In 2001 the band recorded their first demo featuring eight of their best songs - what was it called?

    a) Some of Them X ☐

    b) Be Gone E.P ☐

    c) Legs XI ☐

    d) Shameful Eight ☐

9. Which record label did the band sign with in 2001?

    a) Rough Trade ☐

    b) Creation ☐

    c) Factory ☐

    d) Reprise ☐

10. After signing with the record label Peter and Carl moved to 112a Teeside Street - which they nicknamed "The Albion Rooms" - which area of East London was the flat?

   a) Shoreditch ☐

   b) Whitechapel ☐

   c) Wapping ☐

   d) Bethnal Green ☐

(ANSWERS CAN BE FOUND ON PAGE 72)

SECTION TWO

Up the Bracket 2002

1. Prior to the release of the album the band released a double A-side featuring "What a Waster" and which "Up the Bracket" Album track?

    a) Begging ☐

    b) I Get Along ☐

    c) Tell the King ☐

    d) Horror Show ☐

2. Which former member of Suede produced the double A-side?

    a) Bernard Butler ☐

    b) Brett Anderson ☐

    c) Alex Lee ☐

    d) Mat Osman ☐

3. In February 2002 which American band did The Libertines support?

    a) Red Hot Chili Peppers ☐

    b) Foo Fighters ☐

    c) The Strokes ☐

    d) The White Stripes ☐

4. "Up the Bracket" was released in October 2002 which member of The Clash produced the album?

    a) Joe Strummer ☐

    b) Topper Headon ☐

    c) Paul Simonen ☐

    d) Mick Jones ☐

5. What does the front cover image on the album depict?

    a) A Police Chase ☐

    b) Riot Police ☐

    c) An Angry Mob ☐

    d) A Hospital Room ☐

6. The album title was taken from Tony Hancock - it featured in "Hancock's Half Hour" as a slang term for what?

   a) A Punch in the Throat ☐

   b) A Simple Mind ☐

   c) Downing a Pint ☐

   d) Climbing a flag pole ☐

7. What is the opening track on the album?

   a) Vertigo ☐

   b) Death on the Stairs ☐

   c) Boys in the Band ☐

   d) Radio America ☐

8. What number did it peak at in the UK album charts?

   a) 5 ☐

   b) 20 ☐

   c) 35 ☐

   d) 40 ☐

9. "Time for Heroes" was released as a single in January 2003 - which film does the song feature on the soundtrack of?

    a) Runaway Jury ☐

    b) Identity ☐

    c) Touching the Void ☐

    d) American Wedding ☐

10. The band featured regularly wearing red tunics during this period - what regiment of the British army does the tunic represent?

    a) The Royal Artillery ☐

    b) The Coldstream Guards ☐

    c) The Parachute Regiment ☐

    d) The Grenadier Guards ☐

(ANSWERS CAN BE FOUND ON PAGE 73)

SECTION THREE

Up the Bracket Lyrics

1. Down in the street below, hear the _____ archangel sing

2. It turns you into stone, no I'm reversing down the _____ street

3. Oh, how just to slowly, _____ screw myself to death

4. It's these _____ faces they bring this town down

5. But tell me baby, how does it feel? I know you like the roll of the _____ wheel

6. And all across Africa, China and _____ I will call

7. Saw the same two men on the _____ Road

8. You're like a _____ how you can cut and paste and twist, you're awful

9. New York City's very pretty in the night time, but don't you miss _____

10. All animals we are, round the _____ in the park

11. It's not about tenements and _____

12. Something ain't quite right, you've got the _____ on your side

(ANSWERS CAN BE FOUND ON PAGE 74)

SECTION FOUR

The Libertines 2004

1. Who became manager of the band between the release of the first two albums?

    a) Alan McGee ☐

    b) David Balfe ☐

    c) Malcolm McLaren ☐

    d) Paul McGuiness ☐

2. Prior to this album the band released "Don't Look Back into the Sun" in the music video which store do the band appear to steal their own record from?

    a) WHSmith ☐

    b) Woolworths ☐

    c) HMV ☐

    d) Virgin ☐

3. The album cover features a photograph of Pete and Carl at the 2003 "Freedom Gig" taken at the Tap 'n' Tin Club by which photographer?

   a) Roger Sargeant ☐

   b) Nigel Crane ☐

   c) Roger Crane ☐

   d) Nigel Sargeant ☐

4. Following this performance the band played three consecutive sold-out dates in December at which London venue?

   a) Wembley Arena ☐

   b) Islington Academy ☐

   c) The Forum ☐

   d) Brixton Academy ☐

5. Album track "The Man Who Would Be King"
    takes its title from a short story by which
    author?

    a) Franz Kafka ☐

    b) Rudyard Kipling ☐

    c) Ernest Hemingway ☐

    d) Oscar Wilde ☐

6. What was the first single to be released from
    the album?

    a) Last Post on the Bugle ☐

    b) Can't Stand Me Now ☐

    c) What Became of the Likely Lads ☐

    d) Music When the Lights Go Out ☐

7. In November 2004 the band released a DVD
    of live footage, videos and extras - what was its
    title?

    a) The Likely Lads ☐

    b) The Men Who Would be King ☐

    c) The Ha Ha Wall ☐

    d) Boys in the Band ☐

8. Complete the title of this album track "Road to _____"

    a) Home ☐

    b) Ruin ☐

    c) Rage ☐

    d) Rome ☐

9. What number did the album reach in the UK album charts?

    a) 1 ☐

    b) 5 ☐

    c) 10 ☐

    d) 20 ☐

10. "Arbeit Macht Frei" features in which 2006 film?

    a) The Last King of Scotland ☐

    b) The Da Vinci Code ☐

    c) Children of Men ☐

    d) Blood Diamond ☐

(ANSWERS CAN BE FOUND ON PAGE 75)

The Libertines Lyrics

1. No, you've got it the wrong way round. You shut me up and blamed it on the

   _____

2. I was carried away, caught up in an

   _____

3. For if you are shy for tomorrow, you'll be shy for one _____ days

4. I've been told if you want to make it in this game, you got to have the luck, you got to have the _____

5. And all the memories of the pubs and the clubs and the drugs and the _____ we shared together

6. You wanna be just like them, 'cause they are so _____

7. It's been a long war and I'm _____ and dirty

8. She's cleaning the steps in a mean street, where no _____ walk the beat

9. I tried it with Charlene and I spent three days on my _____

10. Hurry up Mrs _____, I can feel it coming down

11. Fifteen holes in the _____ chest

12. And only fools, _____ and undertakers will have any time for you

13. Dreams are strewn across the sand, you won't need _____

14. But blood runs thicker, oh we're thick as _____ you know

15. The ideal girl in London from _____
(ANSWERS CAN BE FOUND ON PAGE 76)

Peter Doherty in Profile

1. Where in Northumberland was Peter born?

    a) Bamburgh ☐

    b) Morpeth ☐

    c) Berwick ☐

    d) Hexham ☐

2. At the age of 16 Peter won a poetry competition and embarked on a tour to which country? Organised by the British Council

    a) Russia ☐

    b) France ☐

    c) Italy ☐

    d) China ☐

3. What course did Peter study at Queen Mary University of London?

    a) Modern Art ☐

    b) Political Science ☐

    c) English Literature ☐

    d) Politics ☐

4. What football club does Peter support?

a) Fulham ☐

b) Queens Park Rangers ☐

c) West Ham United ☐

d) Chelsea ☐

5. What is Peters nickname?

a) Beaky ☐

b) Beano ☐

c) Biro ☐

d) Bilo ☐

6. In which prison did Doherty serve a one-month sentence in the summer of 2003?

a) Pentonville ☐

b) Belmarsh ☐

c) Wandsworth ☐

d) Brixton ☐

7. In April 2004 Peter recorded vocals on a single called "For Lovers" by which artist?

    a) Werewolf ☐

    b) Wolfman ☐

    c) Wolfie ☐

    d) WhereWolf ☐

8. What is the name of Peters first child with Lisa Moorish?

    a) Astile ☐

    b) Ashanti ☐

    c) Asher ☐

    d) Aspen ☐

9. What is the title of Peters 2023 biographical documentary?

    a) Still the Same, No Change ☐

    b) Looking Down Upon Me ☐

    c) Blank Look in the Mirror ☐

    d) Stranger in My Own Skin ☐

10. What is the name of Peters current wife?

    a) Maria de Felix ☐

    b) Katia de Vidas ☐

    c) Katia de Felix ☐

    d) Maria de Vidas ☐

(ANSWERS CAN BE FOUND ON PAGE 77)

Babyshambles

1. Who was the original drummer for Babyshambles?

   a) Gemma Walters ☐

   b) Joanne Clarke ☐

   c) Joanne Walters ☐

   d) Gemma Clarke ☐

2. What was the title of the bands second single? Released in November 2004

   a) Albion ☐

   b) Killamangiro ☐

   c) Pipedown ☐

   d) Back from the Dead ☐

3. What is the name of the debut Babyshambles album released in 2005?

   a) Albion the Great ☐

   b) Albion my Home ☐

   c) Down in Albion ☐

   d) Out in Albion ☐

4. In September and October 2005 Babyshambles started a 19-date tour - what was the name of the tour?

   a) The Pentonville Rough Tour ☐

   b) The Pipe Down Tour ☐

   c) 8 Dead Boys Tour ☐

   d) Merry Go Round Tour ☐

5. In August 2006 the band released what limited edition single?

   a) Beg, Steal or Borrow ☐

   b) Home Again ☐

   c) Ready, Steady.... ☐

   d) Time for Changes ☐

6. What was the name of the E.P released in December 2006?

   a) You Talk ☐

   b) I Wish ☐

   c) Sedative ☐

   d) The Blinding ☐

7. What is the title of the second Babyshambles album released on 1st October 2007?

    a) There She Goes ☐

    b) Side of the Road ☐

    c) Shotter's Nation ☐

    d) Lost Art of Murder ☐

8. And what was the title of the first single to be released from the album?

    a) You Talk ☐

    b) Delivery ☐

    c) Carry On Up the Morning ☐

    d) French Dog Blues ☐

9. What is the name of the bass player in Babyshambles?

    a) Drew McConnell ☐

    b) Mick Whitnall ☐

    c) James Morrison ☐

    d) Adam Falkner ☐

10. In 2013 the band released their third album entitled what?

   a) Nothing Comes to Nothing ☐

   b) Fall from Grace ☐

   c) Sequel to the Prequel ☐

   d) Seven Shades ☐

(ANSWERS CAN BE FOUND ON PAGE 78)

THE LIBERTINES

Dirty Pretty Things

1. Which UK label released the "Waterloo to Anywhere" album?

   a) Cadillac ☐

   b) Vertigo ☐

   c) Venus ☐

   d) Candid ☐

2. Bass player Didz Hammond left which band to join the Dirty Pretty Things?

   a) The Cooper Temple Clause ☐

   b) Black Rebel Motorcycle Club ☐

   c) Hundred Reasons ☐

   d) Capdown ☐

3. What is the title of the debut Dirty Pretty Things single?

   a) Deadwood ☐

   b) The Enemy ☐

   c) Gin & Milk ☐

   d) Bang Bang, You're Dead ☐

4. What is the title of the bands second album released in 2008?

    a) Love on the Rocks ☐

    b) Romance at Short Notice ☐

    c) Letter to My Friend ☐

    d) Written in the Scars ☐

5. What is the title of the first single released from the album?

    a) Buzzards & Crows ☐

    b) Truth Begins ☐

    c) Tired of England ☐

    d) Faultlines ☐

6. Complete the title of this Dirty Pretty Things album track "The Gentry _____"

    a) Cove ☐

    b) Curve ☐

    c) Cycle ☐

    d) Chain ☐

7. What is the title of the 2006 Dirty Pretty Things DVD recorded live at The Forum?

    a) Smoking in the Toilet ☐

    b) Puffing in the Dark ☐

    c) Final Nail in the Coffin ☐

    d) Puffing on a Coffin Nail ☐

8. Complete the Dirty Pretty Things lyric "Oh, I gave you the Midas touch. Ah, you turn 'round and _____ out my heart"

    a) Tear ☐

    b) Scratch ☐

    c) Burn ☐

    d) Hack ☐

9. Name the title of this Dirty Pretty Things song from the opening lyric "You got the world boy, this all you make it?

    a) Deadwood ☐

    b) Wondering ☐

    c) If You Love a Woman ☐

    d) Truth Begins ☐

10. "Could do with a little more Anthony actually" is spoken at the opening of which album track?

   a) Bang Bang, You're Dead ☐

   b) Deadwood ☐

   c) Doctors and Dealers ☐

   d) Last of the Small Town Playboys ☐

(ANSWERS CAN BE FOUND ON PAGE 79)

Gary Powell in Profile

1. Where was Gary born?

    a) Seattle ☐

    b) Miami ☐

    c) Los Angeles ☐

    d) New York ☐

2. In which area of England did Gary grow up?

    a) Manchester ☐

    b) Birmingham ☐

    c) Bristol ☐

    d) Brighton ☐

3. What is the name of Gary's long-term partner?

    a) Joanne ☐

    b) Jean ☐

    c) Joanie ☐

    d) Jude ☐

4. How many children does Gary have?

    a) One ☐

    b) Two ☐

    c) Three ☐

    d) Five ☐

5. Which British reggae artist has Gary drummed for?

    a) Aswad ☐

    b) Pato Banton ☐

    c) General Levy ☐

    d) Eddy Grant ☐

6. Who did Gary feature on drums for during their 2004 reunion shows?

    a) My Bloody Valentine ☐

    b) A Tribe Called Quest ☐

    c) New York Dolls ☐

    d) P.I.L ☐

7. From 2016-2019 Gary was the touring drummer for which Ska band?

    a) The Beat ☐

    b) The Specials ☐

    c) Madness ☐

    d) Bad Manners ☐

8. What is the name of Gary's record label?

    a) 25 Hour Convenience store ☐

    b) At Your Convenience ☐

    c) Spark Plug Records ☐

    d) Powell Not Cowell ☐

9. Gary has deejayed for club NME at which London venue?

    a) Lord Napier Star ☐

    b) The Good Ship ☐

    c) Scala ☐

    d) Koko ☐

10. What is Gary's middle name?

    a) Peterson ☐

    b) Armstrong ☐

    c) Freeman ☐

    d) Furlong ☐

(ANSWERS CAN BE FOUND ON PAGE 80)

John Hassall in Profile

1. Which school did John attend in North London?

    a) Alleyns School ☐

    b) Kings College School ☐

    c) Highgate School ☐

    d) Latymer Upper School ☐

2. Which band does Hassall refer to as his first love?

    a) The Beatles ☐

    b) The Kinks ☐

    c) The Who ☐

    d) The Rolling Stones ☐

3. What was the name of the band John formed that were active between 2005 and 2009 in which he sang lead vocals?

   a) Iceman ☐

   b) Bigfoot ☐

   c) Snow ☐

   d) Yeti ☐

4. What was the name of the band's debut single that reach number 30 in the UK Charts?

   a) Didn't Think of That ☐

   b) Never Lose Your Sense of Wonder ☐

   c) Wouldn't Be a Problem ☐

   d) Couldn't Take the Strain ☐

5. In February 2006 which band did they support on part of their European Tour?

   a) Oasis ☐

   b) Blur ☐

   c) Franz Ferdinand ☐

   d) The Arctic Monkeys ☐

6. Which song on Anthem for Doomed Youth
   does John take lead vocal?

   a) Barbarians ☐

   b) Dead for Love ☐

   c) Over It Again ☐

   d) Belly of the Beast ☐

7. Where does John Reside?

   a) Aarhus, Denmark ☐

   b) Stockholm, Sweden ☐

   c) Oslo, Norway ☐

   d) Helsinki, Finland ☐

8. What band did John form whilst living here?
   They also supported Pete on his solo tour

   a) The March Hares ☐

   b) The April Rainers ☐

   c) The February Chills ☐

   d) The August Heat ☐

9. What was the name of the band's debut album released in March 2017?

   a) Wheels to Idyll ☐

   b) Cycle to Forgiveness ☐

   c) Turn to the Right ☐

   d) Close the Door ☐

10. What is the name of Johns wife?

   a) Line Hassall Thomsen ☐

   b) Maria Hassall Jorgenson ☐

   c) Marcia Hassall Thomassen ☐

   d) Linda Hassall Johnson ☐

(ANSWERS CAN BE FOUND ON PAGE 81)

Peter Doherty Going Solo

1. Peter featured on which 2006 Streets song?

    a) Dry Your Eyes ☐

    b) When You Wasn't Famous ☐

    c) Never Went to Church ☐

    d) Prangin' Out ☐

2. In July 2008 Peter played his biggest solo gig at which venue?

    a) Brixton Academy ☐

    b) The Forum ☐

    c) The Royal Albert Hall ☐

    d) Wembley Arena ☐

3. What was the name of the album Peter released in 2009?

    a) Waste/Space ☐

    b) Grace/Wastelands ☐

    c) Grace/Faceless ☐

    d) Pace/Haste ☐

4. What single was released a week before the album?

    a) Last of the English Roses ☐

    b) Broken Love Songs ☐

    c) A Little Death Around the Eyes ☐

    d) I Am the Rain ☐

5. What was the title of the second and final single from the album?

    a) Sheepskin Tearaway ☐

    b) Sweet By and By ☐

    c) Broken Love Song ☐

    d) New Love Grows on Trees ☐

6. Which member of Blur features on the album?

    a) Dave Rowntree ☐

    b) Alex James ☐

    c) Damon Albarn ☐

    d) Graham Coxon ☐

7. What is the opening track of the album?

    a) Salome ☐

    b) Palace of Bone ☐

    c) Arcady ☐

    d) 1939 Returning ☐

8. Which song from the album features a writing credit for Carl?

    a) Sheepskin Tearaway ☐

    b) Lady Don't Fall Backwards ☐

    c) Last of the English Roses ☐

    d) A Little Death Around the Eyes ☐

9. Complete the title of this 2015 release by Peter. "Flags of the Old _____"

    a) Regime ☐

    b) Revolution ☐

    c) Monarchy ☐

    d) Kingdom ☐

10. In 2019 Peter released another album entitled "Peter Doherty and the _____ _____" what?

    a) Ne'er DoWells ☐

    b) Puta Madres ☐

    c) Only Fanaticss ☐

    d) Bad Exploits ☐

(ANSWERS CAN BE FOUND ON PAGE 82)

SECTION TWELVE

Carl Barat in Profile

1. What is Carls full birth name?

    a) Carlos Donald Marcus Barat ☐

    b) Carlos Alberto Ashley Barat ☐

    c) Carlos Ashley Raphael Barat ☐

    d) Carlos Ashley Donald Barat ☐

2. In which Hampshire town was Carl born?

    a) Basingstoke ☐

    b) Winchester ☐

    c) Andover ☐

    d) Aldershot ☐

3. What University was Carl studying Drama at before abandoning his course to start the band?

    a) Cambridge ☐

    b) Brunel ☐

    c) Chichester ☐

    d) Oxford ☐

4. What is Pete's nickname for Carl?

    a) Braggings ☐

    b) Blagpus ☐

    c) Biggles ☐

    d) Boggles ☐

5. What is the name of Carls actress -turned-singer sister?

    a) Lucie ☐

    b) Marie ☐

    c) Sandie ☐

    d) Wendie ☐

6. What is the name of Carls partner?

    a) Esther ☐

    b) Edie ☐

    c) Veronica ☐

    d) Pamela ☐

7. How many children does Carl have?

    a) None ☐

    b) Two ☐

    c) Three ☐

    d) Five ☐

8. What was the name of the band Carl played in alongside Tim Burgess, Martin Duffy and Andy Burrows?

    a) The Changes ☐

    b) The Chaps ☐

    c) The Charts ☐

    d) The Chavs ☐

9. Carl was a featured artist on which song as part of the Artists for Grenfell charity group?

    a) All By Myself ☐

    b) Wish You Were Here ☐

    c) The Sound of Silence ☐

    d) Bridge over Troubled Water ☐

10. In 2012 Carl was awarded an honorary doctorate for his contributions to the arts by which university?

    a) University of Winchester ☐

    b) University of London ☐

    c) University of Kent ☐

    d) University of Manchester ☐

(ANSWERS CAN BE FOUND ON PAGE 83)

THE LIBERTINES

SECTION THIRTEEN

Anthems for Doomed Youth 2015

1. "Anthems for Doomed Youth" is taken from a poem by which war poet?

   a) Siegfried Sassoon ☐

   b) Robert Graves ☐

   c) Wilfred Owen ☐

   d) Ivor Gurney ☐

2. What is the opening track on the album?

   a) Fame and Fortune ☐

   b) Heart of the Matter ☐

   c) Iceman ☐

   d) Barbarians ☐

3. What is the name of the first single to be released from the album?

   a) Glasgow Coma Scale Blues ☐

   b) Gunga Din ☐

   c) Heart of the Matter ☐

   d) Fury of Chonburi ☐

4. What number did the album peak at in the UK album charts?

    a) 1 ☐

    b) 3 ☐

    c) 7 ☐

    d) 12 ☐

5. Complete the title of the album track "The _____ Horse"

    a) Kings ☐

    b) Trojan ☐

    c) Milkman's ☐

    d) Legions ☐

6. In 2015 The Libertines played a secret set at Glastonbury after which band pulled out?

    a) Oasis ☐

    b) Coldplay ☐

    c) The Arctic Monkeys ☐

    d) Foo Fighters ☐

7. On the 5th July 2015 the band reformed to headline a concert at which festival?

   a) Isle of Wight ☐

   b) British Summer Time ☐

   c) All Points East ☐

   d) Reading ☐

8. In 2017 who delivered a speech at the start of the bands Prenton Park concert?

   a) Mel Stride ☐

   b) Jacob Rees-Mogg ☐

   c) Jeremy Corbyn ☐

   d) Andrea Leadsom ☐

9. Which special guest joined the band for their 2015 Glastonbury show?

   a) Ed Harcourt ☐

   b) Paul Heaton ☐

   c) Guy Garvey ☐

   d) Badly Drawn Boy ☐

10. On the front cover of the album what is crossed out above the album title?

    a) Hallelujah Day ☐

    b) Forever and a Day ☐

    c) Satisfaction Guaranteed ☐

    d) Present and Correct ☐

(ANSWERS CAN BE FOUND ON PAGE 84)

SECTION FOURTEEN

Anthems for Doomed Youth Lyrics

1. To the thug you can't cultivate, scrubs working by the _____ gate

2. You've been beaten and _____, probably betrayed

3. Like tin soldiers responding to the call, to _____ we will crawl

4. Was it Cromwell or Orwell who first led you to the _____

5. Just say you love me for _____ good reasons

6. Back in London's grey-scotch mist staring up at my _____

7. Outside a _____ on the Charing Cross Road

8. I am no _____ to the coals, I carry them in my soul

9. Riding jokes like _____ horses, of the apocalypse

10. In my cinematic kind, I see battles fought at _____

11. A dream shared and pulled apart; one dream broken by two _____

12. And now she's pulling up outside, the car lights crawling across the _____

(ANSWERS CAN BE FOUND ON PAGE 85)

SECTION FIFTEEN

Carl Barat Going Solo

1. In 2008 which band did Carl tour with and support at Edinburghs Hogmanay celebrations?

    a) Franz Ferdinand ☐

    b) Glasvegas ☐

    c) Travis ☐

    d) Biffy Clyro ☐

2. In 2010 what was the name of the single that was released with Carl featuring as part of supergroup The Bottletop Band?

    a) Britain has Fallen ☐

    b) Europe Folds ☐

    c) The Fall of Rome ☐

    d) Crumbled Empire ☐

3. Carl released his eponymous solo album in
   2010 - what is he holding on the album cover?

   a) A Rose ☐

   b) A Camera ☐

   c) Binoculars ☐

   d) A Mannequin Arm ☐

4. What is the title of the lead single from the
   album?

   a) Run With the Boys ☐

   b) The Fall ☐

   c) Carve My Name ☐

   d) Shadows Fall ☐

5. The album was timed to coincide with the
   release of Carls memoirs - entitled what?

   a) Penny for a Thought ☐

   b) Ha'Penny Splendour ☐

   c) Threepenny Memoirs ☐

   d) A Shilling for a Song ☐

6. Who features on album track "The Fall"?

    a) Miles Kane ☐

    b) Neil Hannon ☐

    c) Ian Brodie ☐

    d) Damon Albarn ☐

7. In 2014 Carl co-wrote "Love is Not on Trial" for whose album entitled "The Dancing Marquis"? He also contributed vocals and guitar to the track

    a) Marc Almond ☐

    b) Midge Ure ☐

    c) Gary Numan ☐

    d) David Bowie ☐

8. What is the name of Carls backing band? Their album was released in February 2015

    a) The Jackals ☐

    b) The Wolves ☐

    c) The Carnivores ☐

    d) The Muzzles ☐

9. And what is the title of the album they released?

    a) Poor Pretty Me ☐

    b) On Your Marks ☐

    c) It Shall Pour ☐

    d) Let it Reign ☐

10. Which historical figures' statue features on the front cover of the album?

    a) Queen Boudicea ☐

    b) Winston Churchill ☐

    c) Napoleon ☐

    d) Nelson ☐

(ANSWERS CAN BE FOUND ON PAGE 86)

All Quiet on the Eastern Esplanade
2024

1. Who produced the album?

    a) Dimitri Tikovoi ☐

    b) Vladimir Tikovoi ☐

    c) Vladimir Popescu ☐

    d) Dimitri Popescu ☐

2. Who directed the video for "Run Run Run"?

    a) Glenn Brown ☐

    b) Alexander Brown ☐

    c) Alexander Stevens ☐

    d) Glenn Stevens ☐

3. What is the location for the "Run Run Run" video?

    a) Margate ☐

    b) London ☐

    c) Paris ☐

    d) Manchester ☐

4. Which actor plays the cab driver in the video?

    a) Graham Bell ☐

    b) Geoff Lee ☐

    c) Geoff Bell ☐

    d) Graham Lee ☐

5. What was the name of the 10-show intimate club tour the band played to celebrate the announcement of the album?

    a) The All-Quiet Tour ☐

    b) The Mustangs Tour ☐

    c) The Albion Sails Tour ☐

    d) The Albionay Tour ☐

6. What number did the album reach in the UK album charts?

    a) 1 ☐

    b) 2 ☐

    c) 5 ☐

    d) 10 ☐

7. Who likes a drinky in the lyrics of Mustangs?

  a) Chloe ☐

  b) Sammy ☐

  c) Traci ☐

  d) Sarah ☐

8. What is the title of the final track on the album?

  a) Be Young ☐

  b) Oh Sh*t ☐

  c) Night of the Hunter ☐

  d) Songs They Never Play on the Radio ☐

9. Complete the title of this album track – "Barons _____"

  a) Stage ☐

  b) Claw ☐

  c) Court ☐

  d) Brown ☐

10. What was the third and final single released from the album in January 2024?

    a) Shiver ☐

    b) Merry Old England ☐

    c) Man With the Melody ☐

    d) I Have a Friend ☐

(ANSWERS CAN BE FOUND ON PAGE 87)

SECTION SEVENTEEN

All Quiet on the Eastern Esplanade Lyrics

1. He's an all-time lover and a _____ man

2. He guzzles up the rider, he's like _____ when he goes

3. And the tears fall like _____ without warning

4. With her chalk cliffs once white, they're greying in the _____ light

5. But I better go, with my _____ in tow

6. I want you when you smile, you got the _____ in your eyes

7. Well don't blame me, it's the _____ that made me

8. They'd just installed the first _____ at the ancestral home

9. The last King of every dying _____

10. You're wondering away, when you're one _____ away

11. As the _____ fall on the old shipping wrecker

(ANSWERS CAN BE FOUND ON PAGE 88)

SECTION EIGHTEEN

Opening Lyric Quiz

Simply write the name of the song that corresponds to the opening lyric.......

1. On the bus the other day, you could tell right from the start

   _____

2. From way far across the sea came an Eritrean maiden

   _____

3. You caught me in the middle, dazed on the carpet

   _____

4. An ending fitting for the start, you twist and tore our love apart

   _____

5. Is it cruel or kind not to speak my mind

_____

6. You'll never fumigate the demons, no matter how much you smoke

_____

7. I know, I know, I know you came the long way 'round

_____

8. (Babyshambles) Why would you pay to see me in a cage?

_____

9. (Dirty Pretty Things) I knew all along that I was right at the start

_____

10. (Peter Doherty) My, you did look dapper in your mother's old green scarf

_____

(ANSWERS CAN BE FOUND ON PAGE 89)

Complete the Title

Complete the title of these Libertines B-Sides, demos and rarities

1. _____ for the 21st Century

2. Skint and _____

3. _____ & Bone man

4. I Love You (But You're _____)

5. 7 _____ Frenchmen

6. Pay the _____

7. _____ Road Lover

8. Love on the _____

9. _____ boys

10. Hooligans on ___

(ANSWERS CAN BE FOUND ON PAGE 90)

ANSWERS

Section One: Early Days

1.   d) The Strand ☐

2.   c) Steve Bedlow ☐

3.   a) Marquis de Sade ☐

4.   d) Johnny Borrell ☐

5.   a) Filthy McNastys ☐

6.   b) Roger Morton ☐

7.   d) Paul Dufour ☐

8.   c) Legs XI ☐

9.   a) Rough Trade ☐

10   d) Bethnal Green ☐

/10

Section Two: Up the Bracket 2002

1.   b) I Get Along ☐

2.   a) Bernard Butler ☐

3.   c) The Strokes ☐

4.   d) Mick Jones ☐

5.   b) Riot Police ☐

6.   a) A Punch in the Throat ☐

7.   a) Vertigo ☐

8.   c) 35 ☐

9.   d) American Wedding ☐

10   b) The Coldstream Guards ☐

/10

Section Three: Up the Bracket Lyrics

1. Drunken ☐
2. Lonely ☐
3. Sharply ☐
4. Ignorant ☐
5. Limousine ☐
6. Australia ☐
7. Cally ☐
8. Journalist ☐
9. Soho ☐
10. Bench ☐
11. Needles ☐
12. Devil ☐

/12

Section Four: The Libertines 2004

1.   a)   Alan McGee ☐
2.   d)   Virgin ☐
3.   a)   Roger Sargeant ☐
4.   c)   The Forum ☐
5.   b)   Rudyard Kipling ☐
6.   b)   Can't Stand Me Now ☐
7.   d)   Boys in the Band ☐
8.   b)   Ruin ☐
9.   a)   1 ☐
10   c)   Children of Men ☐

/10

Section Five: The Libertines Lyrics

1. Brown ☐
2. Affray ☐
3. Thousand ☐
4. Look ☐
5. Tubs ☐
6. Cool ☐
7. Tired ☐
8. Policemen ☐
9. Back ☐
10. Brown ☐
11. Dealers ☐
12. Vultures ☐
13. Money ☐
14. Thieves ☐
15. France ☐

/15

Section Six: Peter Doherty in Profile

1. d) Hexham ☐
2. a) Russia ☐
3. c) English Literature ☐
4. b) Queens Park Rangers ☐
5. d) Bilo ☐
6. c) Wandsworth ☐
7. b) Wolfman ☐
8. a) Astile ☐
9. d) Stranger in My Own Skin ☐
10 b) Katia de Vidas ☐

/10

Section Seven: Babyshambles

1. d) Gemma Clarke ☐
2. b) Killamangiro ☐
3. c) Down in Albion ☐
4. b) The Pipe Down Tour ☐
5. a) Beg, Steal or Borrow ☐
6. d) The Blinding ☐
7. c) Shotter's Nation ☐
8. b) Delivery ☐
9. a) Drew McConnell ☐
10. c) Sequel to the Prequel ☐

/10

Section Eight: Dirty Pretty Things

1   b)   Vertigo ☐

2   a)   The Cooper Temple Clause ☐

3   d)   Bang Bang, You're Dead ☐

4   b)   Romance at Short Notice ☐

5   c)   Tired of England ☐

6   a)   Cove ☐

7   d)   Puffing on a Coffin Nail ☐

8   b)   Scratch ☐

9   a)   Deadwood ☐

10 a)   Bang Bang, You're Dead ☐

/10

Section Nine: Gary Powell in Profile

1.   c)   Los Angeles ☐

2.   b)   Birmingham ☐

3.   d)   Jude ☐

4.   b)   Two ☐

5.   d)   Eddy Grant ☐

6.   c)   New York Dolls ☐

7.   b)   The Specials ☐

8.   a)   25 Hour Convenience store ☐

9.   d)   Koko ☐

10.   b)   Armstrong ☐

/10

Section Ten: John Hassall in Profile

1. c) Highgate School ☐

2. a) The Beatles ☐

3. d) Yeti ☐

4. b) Never Lose Your Sense of Wonder ☐

5. a) Oasis ☐

6. c) Over It Again ☐

7. a) Aarhus Denmark ☐

8. b) The April Rainers ☐

9. a) Wheels to Idyll ☐

10. a) Line Hassall Thomsen ☐

/10

Section Eleven: Peter Doherty Going Solo

1   d)   Prangin' Out ☐
2   c)   The Royal Albert Hall ☐
3   b)   Grace/Wastelands ☐
4   a)   Last of the English Roses ☐
5   c)   Broken Love Song ☐
6   d)   Graham Coxon ☐
7   c)   Arcady ☐
8   d)   A Little Death Around the Eyes ☐
9   a)   Regime ☐
10 b)   Puta Madres ☐

/10

Section Twelve: Carl Barat in Profile

1   c)   Carlos Ashley Raphael Barat ☐

2   a)   Basingstoke ☐

3   b)   Brunel ☐

4   c)   Biggles ☐

5   a)   Lucie ☐

6   b)   Edie ☐

7   b)   Two ☐

8   d)   The Chavs ☐

9   d)   Bridge over Troubled Water ☐

10 a)   University of Winchester ☐

/10

Section Thirteen: Anthems for Doomed Youth 2015

1 c) Wilfred Owen ☐

2 d) Barbarians ☐

3 b) Gunga Din ☐

4 b) 3 ☐

5 c) Milkman's ☐

6 d) Foo Fighters ☐

7 b) British Summer Time ☐

8 c) Jeremy Corbyn ☐

9 a) Ed Harcourt ☐

10 a) Hallelujah Day ☐

/10

Section Fourteen: Anthems for Doomed Youth Lyrics

1. Prison ☐
2. Flayed ☐
3. Camden ☐
4. Stairwell ☐
5. Three ☐
6. Therapist ☐
7. Bookshop ☐
8. Stranger ☐
9. Trojan ☐
10. Sea ☐
11. Libertines ☐
12. Curtain ☐

/12

Section Fifteen: Carl Barat Going Solo

1 b) Glasvegas ☐

2 c) The Fall of Rome ☐

3 b) A Camera ☐

4 a) Run With the Boys ☐

5 c) Threepenny Memoirs ☐

6 b) Neil Hannon ☐

7 a) Marc Almond ☐

8 a) The Jackals ☐

9 d) Let it Reign ☐

10 a) Queen Boudicea ☐

/10

Section Sixteen: All Quiet on the Eastern Esplanade 2024

1 a) Dimitri Tikovoi ☐

2 b) Alexander Brown ☐

3 a) Margate ☐

4 c) Geoff Bell ☐

5 d) The Albionay Tour ☐

6 a) 1 ☐

7 c) Traci ☐

8 d) Songs They Never Play on the Radio ☐

9 b) Claw ☐

10 a) Shiver ☐

/10

Section Seventeen: All Quiet on the Eastern Esplanade Lyrics

1. Marathon ☐
2. Pac-Man ☐
3. Bombs ☐
4. Sodium ☐
5. Demons ☐
6. Dollars ☐
7. World ☐
8. Phone ☐
9. Empire ☐
10. Degree ☐
11. Cobwebs ☐

/11

Section Eighteen: Opening Lyric Quiz

1. The Delaney ☐
2. Death on the Stairs ☐
3. I Get Along ☐
4. Can't Stand Me Now ☐
5. Music When the Lights Go Out ☐
6. You're My Waterloo ☐
7. Merry Old England ☐
8. Killamangiro ☐
9. Bang Bang, You're Dead ☐
10. The Last of the English Roses ☐

/10

Section Nineteen: Complete the Title

1. Hooray ☐
2. Minted ☐
3. Skag ☐
4. Green ☐
5. Deadly ☐
6. Lady ☐
7. Breck ☐
8. Dole ☐
9. Dilly ☐
10. E ☐

/10

That completes the quiz and with a total of 200 points available – where do you stand?

175-200 A Lust for The Libertines

150-174 Begging to Be King

125-149 Right at the Heart of the Matter

101-124 Room for Improvement

51-100 Still learning the chords

0-50 What a Waster!

Hopefully you have enjoyed this little quiz book and it has been a challenge but your knowledge has extended and been rewarded. Now it's time to challenge your friends and family.

Take away multiple choice options for the easier questions and use the book to teach the next generation of fans about the history of this great band.

Printed in Great Britain
by Amazon

49821477R00056